The Future Has a Reputation

The Future Has a Reputation

Poems by Susanna Kittredge

CW Books

Published by CW Books
P.O. Box 541106
Cincinnati, OH 45254-1106

ISBN: 978-1-62549-336-1

Poetry Editor: Kevin Walzer
Business Editor: Lori Jareo

Visit us on the web at www.readcwbooks.com

Cover photo by Jeffrey Hayashida
Author photo by Shelby Meyerhoff

Acknowledgements

I am grateful to the editors of the following journals, in which these poems first appeared:

Barrow Street: "think about your instrument size"

The Columbia Review: "The Cajun Waltz"

Shampoo: "on disgruntle to westminster"

Sixfold: "Four Theories About My Ovaries," "Medusa," "Apology," and "My Heart"

We Still Like: "Quake"

Thanks

Big thanks to the Jamaica Pond Poets and The Brighton Word Factory. I am so lucky to have these two groups who nurture and inspire my writing.

Thanks also to my professors and fellow students from the Master of Fine Arts in Creative Writing program at San Francisco State University.

Finally, thanks to Jeff Hayashida and Shelby Meyerhoff for their cover and author photographs.

Poem Notes

The three "Odes" in this book are based on Frank O'Hara's poem "V.R. Lang."

Lowercase titles were taken from the subject lines of spam emails.

While many of these poems are based on true events, others are pure flights of fancy. For instance, unlike the father in "Cajun Waltz," mine has never had a heart attack; and my real-life in-laws are to be reassured that the characters in "My Husband" have nothing to do with them.

*To my parents for their love and support,
and to Brendan for the same.*

Table of Contents

I. This New Year

This New Year.. 15

The Cajun Waltz.. 16

Summer Camp... 17

heave your beloved night time................................. 19

migratory inconvenient... 20

Chopped Liver.. 21

Vertigo By Proxy.. 22

Andrew... 24

What will we do with you, Monique?........................... 25

valiant no sandpaper.. 26

Georgie.. 27

Snow... 28

Shipwrecked.. 29

II. The Future

Ode (for Frank O'Hara)... 35

Good Friday.. 36

her bullfinch a redactor....................................... 38

think about your instrument size.............................. 40

"What's Really in Those Boxes?".............................. 42

Trap... 43

Abecedarian for Dinah.. 44

Stingray Sings.. 46

Poems My Friend Sam Told Me to Write......................... 47

Instructions To The Friends Who Will Be Staying In My Room
    While I Am Away.. 48

Left Arm... 50

Aging at the Literary Salon.................................... 51

Ode (for Beth)... 52

Where Do You See Yourself In The Future?..................... 53

The Goat.. 54
Big Like Mountains.. 55

III. My Heart
Bring me a Towel.. 63
My Heart... 64
Four Theories About My Ovaries............................... 65
Medusa... 67
Hangover.. 68
Astrology I.. 69
be bunny he burly.. 70
Apology.. 72
Astrology II.. 73
on disgruntle to westminster..................................... 74
for reptilian or nutcrack... 76
Hither.. 78
Moving In... 79
My Husband.. 81
Dream Life.. 83
Love... 84
Quake... 85
Ode (for Brendan).. 93

I. This New Year

This New Year

Open this new year like a letter, written
by a Serbo-Croatian poet with mysterious diacritics
over the consonants of his name.

Take your time with your translation,
each iteration more complex, month by month.
Whenever you learn something new—
about your nephew's strange love of numbers,
the guile of your city councilman,
the chemistry of the lightning bug's tail—
translate this letter again.

Ponder its opening sentences when you are tired and muted.
Tackle it four paragraphs at a time in the afterglow of exercise.
And when you think you might be in love, sound out three words
over and over until they become your mantra, a gift
to your self-most self.

Your translation will never be complete. Not
on December thirty-first when you've deciphered
the final eyelet of the signature; not when the post-scripts
trail off well into the following April; not even
on your deathbed, your manuscript of faded correspondence,
rife with marginalia.

The Cajun Waltz

My father never taught me to do a Cajun Waltz.
Or if he did, I was too young to remember.
He was particularly handsome and disposed
to heart attacks.

The funerals get fatter with the ghosts
of what we believed in: eat right—the salmon,
the fiber—pull yourself out of bed. Run.

I say, do three months' worth of eating while swaying
your hips like a big truck in a strong wind.
Cook. Eat like an omnivore. Dare yourself
to walk away.

Summer Camp

It is the original era of my being. Who am I?
I am twelve years old and my tiny freckles are scattered
around. I'm afraid of nothing, and everything. Girls
can interpret dreams, shape each other's brows.

Lucy grows like a wild plant. A cactus-like
plant. She tries out her *voice* with considerable difficulty.
This sound disturbs and blinds us. It is
like a few shattered pines reconciling two shades
of black. She decides that we are certain
about who we are, and locks herself in clairvoyance.

There are cupcakes. Texture is key. There is no cure
for a very moist interior with a delicate crumb.
Don't laugh to my face without these thoughts.

We love how cute the right heel
or handbag in the un-tuned instruments
of our eyes and what we ignore, we say,
is our personal concerns; entrenched in our kinship
with others. We always have this choice.

Frame the beach, the ember remnants
of a campfire, escape from who others are.
They are sleeping. I go outside and into the lake.
I am tempted. The facts of life. We have groomed
each other and our every mood.

heave your beloved night time

For hours the sun has gathered momentum through its transit
across the underside of the earth and now
heaves your beloved night over the prow of horizon.

Each night is an injured thing—prickled by stars or smothered in fog—
and the injured part of you finds it sympathetic.
In sleep, you and night are of a piece.

Even now in the dawn, in your own mind you are undifferentiated
from the sheets and blankets, from the shirt that you have cast
across your eyes to trap night against them just a little longer;

but the daylight, pushing its fingers between the blind-slats,
finds you, and you are forced to pull yourself upright
and be distinct.

migratory inconvenient

My dear Revisionist,
the leaves are falling here
without fanfare, air a little crisp.
In July a fledgling band-tailed pigeon was found
knocking down trees, or rather
road crews were knocking down trees
when they stumbled
over the Federal Migratory Bird Act.

The large, chunky dove, technically
a partial migrant, loves
its well-worn paths up and down the coast.
Yours are more erratic.

Fall has come, the felling can resume,
and you have managed to knock me
flat on my back once again.
In your dove gray sweater with a stripe
around your middle, I'll call you my own
columba fasciata.

You are migratory, inconvenient,
rewriting your motives over and over,
leaving half-cut branches to dangle
between California seasons,
yellow, green, and gold.

Chopped Liver

What am I, chopped liver? A cow's or chicken's filter
spread on rye in your uncle Ira's deli?

You say you hate knots, but what am I, then,
a Boy Scout tangling his thumbs in lengths of clothesline
for a hopeless badge?

What am I to you, a body poem? A tale, told by a bad slam girl,
full of belly and breastbone, signifying nothing?

What am I, catatonic calligraphy? The guided scrawling
of an oblivious hand turned Ouija board for a message
from your own sick psyche?

Really, what am I, a ghostly reflection? Some weak light
ricocheting between a body and a plate glass window
in a dumb fake of a haunting?

What am I, mythical? Sharing my own body
with that of horse or fish? Ancient and distorted?
Failing to exist?

Vertigo By Proxy

"Skyscrapers, electrical towers, monuments—if it's tall and dangerous looking, teens in Russia are climbing it to capture some breathtaking shots."
Katherine Brooks for the Huffington Post, 6 May, 2012

The young daredevil Kirill Oreshkin is balanced—
one foot, one hand—on the ridges of my esophagus.
Coy dark eyes, small modest smile.
The crowd gathered under my skin does the wave
every time he shifts position and does not plunge
to the acid bath below.
He likes the views, he says. The fear is gone.
Then deftly he pulls himself up to the safety
of my mouth, his brown hair tousled by my exhale,
relief.

But the suspense isn't over. Kirill turns his camera
toward a friend who calls himself Mustang: one arm hooked
over my epiglottis, he hangs with his free hand posed
behind his head, brazen grin, legs pulled up as if a magic carpet,
and not his own audacity, was holding him aloft.
Sometimes, he thinks about something else—
his cat, a salad. (Not his poor mother. Not
my own propensity for ulcers).

Finally, Mustang, too, gets bored of certain death
and plants his sneakers firmly next to Kirill's on my tongue.
The two stride down that astounded, lolling carpet,
both of them alive. More alive and brave and foolish
than this body, their stage.

Andrew

He could not find his book last night which is why
but realizes now—yes, this makes sense—it is probably
under the couch and he will find it diligently tonight, he will
finish the work tonight. Definitely. Yes.
Or his mother insisted that he finish his chores and it took longer
than expected because, and then his little brother
always hogs the computer, he's sure he put it
in his binder but the binder is broken and
his parents were having a dinner party and he couldn't concen-
trate he couldn't his desk, he keeps it clean! and his pencils
and the hamsters, so he had to change the litter in their
driveway and the bus was late, it was so super early
that he had to run he had to run and the wind
was blowing so hard the leaves were in his face and
everywhere and the sand and he is picking them up and holding
them down and sweeping them into the cyclone that swallows
him up that daily swallows him up
and spits him out again.

What will we do with you, Monique?

Your excuses are as tangled as your hair, yet
you cry and cry to your parents about all the work
you are avoiding anyway.

I love the smile you give me when I reach you
on a channel to your distant planet but then
I lose you again in a static haze.

You are doing yesterday's homework
in pink highlighter because all the pens
and pencils drifted off beyond our atmosphere.

You are placing it in the wrong folder
where it will disintegrate to moon dust
before you find it again.

You are walking out the door,
leaving books and papers and me
floating in your zero gravity wake.

valiant no sandpaper

Scratching at tree trunks, she
"is valiant, no sandpaper." Won't take yes
for an answer, is wed to Maybe, and
never jam today.

Pushes hair from her face,
blue-green lichen caked
beneath her fingernails.

Her finger tips are just a little sore.
The fine lines in her palm shift and spread.

She admires hatchets, their force and weight,
their worn smooth handles, but
will not touch one. Heavy, aren't they,
and dangerous; fit faster in firmer hands.

She calls the tree "ambition," a silly pet name,
and laughs. Its bark is rough and stoic.

Her cat is mewing from a crux of branches twelve feet up
and she is waiting, patiently,
for it to descend.

Georgie

Poor gangly brainbox boy,
all fish eyes and alfalfa,
can't hear the indignant panic of his own voice.

His words are filling a basketless balloon
which strains against the classroom ceiling,
perplexed by the absence of sky.

Snow

The boy's house looks like any other, but no matter what his parents do,
they can't keep the snow from falling out of the cloudy white ceiling.
They have been wading through it for months. It's up
to his father's knees, his mother's thighs. They shovel out
a path for their son while he's sleeping.
They don't want him to know how hard they work against the snow.

Sometimes, after they've collapsed into bed,
the boy wakes up and tiptoes into their room.
He brushes the flakes off their faces,
breathes a little warmth onto their chapped cheeks and fingers.

In the morning when his father wakes him for school,
he pretends to feel safe under his thick white blanket.
Sometimes, he refuses to get up and go outside
where the sky is blue and the ground is black with mud.

Shipwrecked

In our shipwrecked days, we drank
from Athenian amphorae that we rescued
from ancient decks, triumphantly,
no audience except our own egos, our own
manic, thirsty instincts.

We drank the briny vinegar that once was wine,
making ourselves sick and unhappy, then
tied the jugs to trees to collect the water
of the typhoons that kept us cowering
in high-ground caves.

In our shipwrecked days, we did not know
what sleep was. We didn't quite know waking
either, just a hazy consciousness that flickered
in and out.

We both knew that coconuts do not fall hard
and hairy from the trees to knock the memories
out of your head. After the typhoons, we corked
the amphorae and collected coconuts
from the ground.

We sat on the beach sawing with seashells
at their heavy green husks for hours.

Then, taking after gulls, we hurled
the tufted brown shells against the rocks,
weeping like typhoons until
they split open and we gurgled
with satisfaction. We sharpened our fingernails
and picked at the sweet white nutmeat
until the sun turned red.

II. The Future

Ode

for Frank O'Hara

You are so glinting, as if
silverware fought in your letters
or you had to swim through
the iridescent streets of the city
to get to poetry.

You scribble about your friends because you
love them. As if it weren't bad
enough that you cry in the snow
and sing like orcas, I
have to think you are a great humanist!

And you drive nonchalantly by on your
doomed beach buggy, a radiant, naked prince.
Thinking it a great joke. Looking
suddenly alone. But you are here
again, pulling heartbreaking language out of our everyday.

Remember, a dead poet hero
is full of fable. Be always life-like,
full of snot and guile and indecision. Oh
cruise New York in saffron cabs, be happy!
And with your words on, because it rains.

Good Friday

For today, Jesus is dead, and the church
is a somber place.
No celebration here, no singing or even
Eucharist. Christ's body-bread,
in its brass platter, is instated
on a filing cabinet in the church office.

Choir practice has been moved
to the church office.
The singers are surprised to see the Host there,
ready to listen in. They genuflect
and take their places, but
St. Dave the Evangelist is appalled.
How could they think of singing in the presence
of one so recently nailed, flogged,
forsaken and entombed?
How dare they warble "He is risen, Allelu!"
when Jesus is still flat and silent, waiting patiently
for the vigil that will urge him back.

"Forgive us Lord!" cries St. Dave. Picking up
the plate with trembling hands, he passes it
to a stunned soprano, saying:

Bring Jesus to the lavatory and set him gently
on the paper towel dispenser. Run the water
to drown the sound of our premature joy.

her bullfinch a redactor

Her bullfinch a redactor, preparing proclamations. He knows
when the ground moves. His silver cage swings and he sings:

"Wheeeeeee! The earth-bound world comes to an end!
Only the airborne will survive!"
Omits clause after clause of prophecy, because
what is *seismic retrofit*? Why should anything escape but him?

Feed him a poisoned honeycake,
destroy his image.

He admires his black head in the little mirror,
gives his reflection a beaky kiss, preens
the feathers of his white rump.

She puts a blanket over his cage to quiet him, does not
want him overexcited, loves him despite his egomania.
Pitiful thing—he has never lived in open air,
and lacks strength against wind.

If freed by disaster, most likely he would light
on a pale roof to smooth his feathers,
easy prey for the hawk

who would dismember him with a magnificent hooked beak
the likes of which he had never seen before.

think about your instrument size

Tuba or piccolo?

Imagine you are an ant crawling through the labyrinth
of your French horn
encountering corrosion, saliva,
alkaline scent.

Think about the size of your utensils
my spoon is too big;
chopsticks tapered too thin to grasp
a ramen noodle.

Think about the size of your instruments
of destruction—the enemy's alleged cache,
your own tight-target bombs,
shock, awe.

Think about your implement size.
Can you heft it? Keep it held above your head
for a slow count of ten?
Will it cut through a redwood or the stem of a poppy?
Will it get between the gaps in your teeth?

Think about the size of your instrumental
case. How vast and varied is your grammatical declension?

The Russian language carries the "with"
of *I sewed it up with a needle and thread*
in suffixes strung to "needle" and "thread."

Think about the size of agency, use;
the things we carry, and why.

How large is the air in your empty hands?

"What's *Really* in Those Boxes?"

After an article of the same title by John Ombelets, Northeastern
Magazine, *Spring 2016*

We need to be smarter, John Ombelets.
Whip up fear about red and yellow building blocks
on the great gray sea.
Right now, we're like a former Coast Guard officer
looking for his keys on a cruiser.
Like a gaping hole.

Name brand sneakers turn into a dirty bomb,
leveling Chicago and the world's economy.
Terrorist protocols fill the vacuum
of our own, the ones we lost while
mesmerized by waves.

The ocean—it's so big*!* says the House Committee
on Transportation and Infrastructure.
The ocean is on a global scale!

We know! say the loading cranes,
looking exactly like Trojan horses.

Trap

My mechanic found bones under
my hood (chicken, pig);
and small black droppings
(rat picnic, rat latrine)
but no gnawed wires
that he could see. No explanation
for my touchy dash lights.
His only advice: "be careful, deah."

I set traps, but all I caught was
bananas, in various states of unpeel.
(Banana playground, banana night club.)

Rats are clever little bastards.
Rats know not to trust food
they didn't have to dig for.

Bananas see a cage
and walk right in.

Abecedarian for Dinah

About this golden-eyed,
Black fur-monster observing me from the
Corner. It will not eat
Dandelion greens, carrots, or
Escarole, but chows
Ferociously on little fishy niblets
Green with algae or envy.

Hello, hand with no food.
I am not so interested in scritches, so
Just stay still, stop teasing,
'K? and don't
Look at me too long or I'll
Make myself invisible. Got a
Night cloak behind the
Ottoman, under the sofa, and I
Preen in private. Be
Quiet. Noise makes me scatter,
Rattle,
Skulk.
Tomorrow I'll need to meet you again. But,
Understand: I'm not always
Vexed.
With my innate
Xenophobia,

You must think me uncouth; but I'm no
Zealot; I can learn love.

Stingray Sings

At the Casa Blanca Aquarium, you will see posters for the evening lounge act, "Stingray Sings." Under the title is an image of Stingray in his ruby red dress and fake eyelashes, one wing wrapped around a microphone held to his long, flat mouth, open just enough to show hints of his jagged little teeth.

You'll stand in line outside the auditorium, gazing at a brokeback fountain cluttered with greening pennies. The line is slow and stuffy, your nose abused by a stranger's cologne.

But then you take your seat, the lights go up, and there is Stingray, his scarlet gown floating gracefully around him in his glittering tank. He starts a saucy little number called "I am Trouble" and twitches his stinger like a confusingly wet dream.

Later, back in his hotel tank, you'll ask him how he got into this business. "Elementary, my dear flotsam," he'll say, brushing your damp hair from your face with a dexterous fin, "I was born a star."

Poems My Friend Sam Told Me to Write

My friend Sam says I should write a poem about Hawaii—the fat grains of sand. Sam says I should write about the egg-shaped setting sun—the way it stretches to meet the horizon, then oozes out of sight while we look for parking, leaving just an afterthought of pink sky over Waikiki. Sam says I could write a poem about Duke Kahanamoku, the lei-laden arms of whose bronze effigy outstretch towards white men and women tromping the strip in flip flops and board shorts.

When Beth and Sam and I go swimming, I float on my back and ask for a rock and an oyster. Beth brought us here—this ought to be her poem. But Sam says I should write about otters. The way they are little water dog people. The way silver sheaths of air cling to their fur when they dive.

Sam is not a poet. He does something with computers—I don't know exactly what, and that's a shame. Sam tosses the hair out of his eyes and says "sorry, what were you saying?" Sam tells me I should write a poem about Legos—the way we all have them in common. The way they interlock to make awkward little cities. The idea of a brightly colored city.

Sam never said I should write a poem about *him*, but this is what he gets for telling me what to do.

Instructions To The Friends Who Will Be Staying In My Room While I Am Away

I hope you like my bed. It is soft, and loving,
and will hold you when you need to be held.
Treat it well. Fluff its pillows gently before you leave for work,
and be sure to tell it any little compliments that come to mind—
about the suppleness of its mattress, or the clean,
simple lines of its walnut-colored frame.

Feel free to use our kitchen. It is true that the stove works
with a limp—its right front burner is slow to catch—
but use it gently. Do not curse or speak harshly in its presence.
Stroke its smooth white corners and grasp its dials tenderly
between your thumb and forefinger. It has faithfully
cooked for me many a stew and omelet,
and it will do the same for you.

Before you go to bed, leave offerings—
a slice of banana or overripe peach for the fruit flies,
an open box of cereal in the cool corner of the pantry
for the grain moths,
a dollop of peanut butter beside the trash bin
for our tiny gray mice.

Sadly, I must tell you that my roommate Melinda cannot be trusted.
Though her eyes are wide and doe-like, and her voice is honey sweet,

it is clear that she has been using my shampoo.
Keep your shampoo hidden, so that Melinda will not be tempted.
Never leave it in the shower, glistening with errant lather.

The shower: Turn the faucet to nine o'clock, or ten if the weather
has gotten cool. These are also the times when the shower
is at its best. True, it will rinse you with its charming, modest water
at any time of day or night, but between nine and ten PM
the shower can concentrate completely on the state of your hair,
the needs of your skin.
It will reacquaint you with your cleanest, truest self so that you
will feel completely worthy of another night
in the embrace of my generous bed.

Left Arm

I lie mostly on my left arm. The right one
falls asleep like *that*. Like a kitten. Wakes up
confused and fuzzy.

The left arm stays true, more or less. Knows
what it's doing, more or less. When I wake up
on my left arm, I can reach out with my right,
feel around for the snooze button, my glasses, the lamp;
knock over a glass of water which gets me on both feet
hissing incoherent curses, stumbling

toward the bathroom and the paper towels, shaking
the pins and needles from my left hand, because
I lied—sometimes the left nods off too, when tucked
beneath the heavy comfort of my body.

Aging at the Literary Salon

We remove our shoes at the door. Jane's feet
are magnificently swollen. If she is bothered
by the way names and faces slide around
in her memory, she doesn't show it. She crosses
her elephantine ankles and recites a beautiful poem
while her husband listens intently, folded over
at the shoulders, nodding off.

Elizabeth is young, but she reads with a slight twitch
of the head that sets her earrings glinting in the light;
when she is Jane's age, her affectation may become
a Parkinsonian wobble. Andrew's gut will rest
like a sea turtle on his lanky frame; Corrie's lacy bones
will show through her clothes; and David's thick black hair
will recede like a tide, his eyes still as beautiful
as beach stones beneath the rheum,
his forefinger pointing obliquely toward a thought.

When we are old enough to feel our tendons everywhere we walk;
when, from time to time, we cannot taste our food or remember
names we've known for years, what will we have earned?
Wisdom, perhaps. Experience. A cushion for our swollen feet.
A place in the holy bosom of decay.

Ode

for Beth

You are so sunny, as if
copper rang in your veins
or you had to squeeze past
the tough furnace of the boiler room
to get to sleep.

You dream about your mitochondria because you
interrogate them. As if it weren't strange enough
that you lie in palpitations
and churn like seaweed, we
have to imagine you are great ship!

and we float pensively by on our
flimsy hearts, like ruffled red ducks.
Thinking ourselves inadequate persons. Feeling
perfectly lucky. But you are smiling
again, squeezing thick friendship past your body.

Remember, a solid, uncooperative body
is full of person. Be always self-like,
full of smarts and love and hospitality. Oh
go naked in a fuchsia sweater, be happy!
and with my admiration on, because it rains.

Where Do You See Yourself In The Future?

In the future, I see myself with a husband and kids,
great job, leadership role in my colony on Mars.

The future has a reputation for being in outer space,
even though there's not much reason to believe
it won't be just as earth-bound as all the pasts
that were futures once.

Don't you hate it when you're lying in bed
and you notice that you're starting to fall asleep,
and that realization brings you fully back
into consciousness? That's what the future
is like. You'll be going along, just doing the usual,

and suddenly you notice that it's not March anymore,
it's April, and that thing that you were worried
about getting done is not only done
but forgotten about and for just a moment,
you're *there* in the *future* and you savor that moment
until the last of it has dissolved and you are
settled once again in the present,
right here on Earth with your boyfriend
and your cat.

The Goat

I thought a poem last night in bed,
something about a goat and an apple?
I just know it was brilliant.
I wanted to get up and write but the blankets
had me pinned down, whispering
"Shushhh. You'll remember it
in the morning. How could you forget
a poem as beautiful as this?"

But now the words are gone
and all I can see is the rough field
of grass and thistle and the rough,
dumb goat standing there
with its rear toward me, its head
turned slightly to the right as it tries to remember why
it picked up the sweet, shiny, red thing in its mouth and what
it was going to do next.

Big Like Mountains

With the heat wave over, it finally feels like fall
again; like I'll fall down on the job or fall
in love, or fall ill, or fall in with the wrong crowd.
Lose footing on the Fort Funston cliffs and fall into the ocean.

The thing I like about the ocean is that it is really big. So vast
and unknowable. That ounce-upon-gallon of water
can multiply itself to near abstraction.

One thing I like about fall is how the crisp air seems to go on forever.

Leaves fall with little fanfare here. The sycamores'
turn ungracious brown, fly in through my office windows.
I pick them up off the carpet, toss them outside,
and they blow back in again.
A battle with fall. Fall is a battlefield.
Men in Civil War uniforms falling
into a final bed of tough brown leaves.
"If only this battle had been fought in New England,"
they think, "how much more colorful the backdrop
to our deaths!"

Fall foliage at the base of a New Hampshire mountain.
One thing I like about mountains is that they are really big.
That if you fall off them, you fall very, very far. It is a bit like flying

which is like being in all the air, everywhere.

The thing I like about falling is how I start to see things
from just behind my breastbone.

I have dreams about falling, and about flying.
My airplane is low, nearly scraping the buildings.

My favorite thing about dreams is how big they are. How vast
and unknowable. How they can stun us with
secret passages hidden in the walls of our minds.

A thing I like about sleep is how it happens to us
when we are unconscious—a darkness that is vast and unknowable,
eyes moving rapidly beneath their lids.

The thing I like about God is how big He is. How vast
and unknowable. How He is like the ocean, full
of messy kelp beds and underwater volcanoes.
How He knows each whale and tiny krill that swim through Him
and still allows the one to eat the other.

One thing I like about poems is how they go on forever
deep, deep, deep below the page.

A woman came up to me today and said:
"Susanna, this poem is so wonderful, but where

are the people?"

Ah yes, the people.

The thing I like about the earth's population
is how big it is. How it will smother us in ourselves.

The thing I like about people is how human we are,
so full of blood and love and anguish.
How well we make the most of being trapped inside our skins.

Life is so big. It is so unlike a movie,
even when movie music is in our ears and we try desperately
to play to the absent camera. The thing I like
about people is how we try to play to the absent camera,
as if to make ourselves big enough
to fill a silver screen.

One thing I like about mountains is that we can't
always scale them; that mountain goats have us beat.

Mountains aspire towards the sky and past it.
When the clouds cut off the ground from their view,
the mountains think that they have succeeded in breaking
through the sky
until night falls, and they see that the stars are no closer.
Nighttime is so dark and star-pricked. So vast, and unknowable.

And Orion seems to have lain sideways in the sky
millions of miles away for millions of years.

One thing I like about this poem is that it is getting quite long.
(How terrifying to think that it could go on forever and become
very long and boring and terrible.)

(How terrifying to look up past the mountain
into the night sky towards Orion
and think about the billions of miles the light has fallen
to reach us.)

One thing I like about outer space is how impossible it is,
so vast and unknowable and made of nothing;
how we will never, ever reach its edge.

III. My Heart

Bring me a Towel

This poem's title has gotten soggy in a tidal
pool of tilde—all the squirming diacriticals breed here
uncritically in saline typographical Eros: umlauts, semicolons
and arrows (dash, dash, greater-than).

Text me back with a less-than-symbol number-three;
more days than that and we might stink like fish and houseguests.
Absence makes the heart grow fondler, caressing the "you"
within its muscular ventricles that trickle with raw red love.

"You" likes that, doesn't "you."

There is no question mark at the end of that sentence.
The question marks are busy curly-Q-ing their way
around the exclamation points at that aforementioned shore-side
orgy. Through pilcrow's prosey pillowtalk and period's wild red run,

the "I" is eyeing you's blush-paused commas,
savoring the receding wink of ellipses
with an oblong smile.

My Heart

is a slowly dripping popsicle
visited only by half-starved hummingbirds
and nervous brown butterflies.

My heart is a traffic island, terrified
by the honking cars around it;
too stunned to comfort the wild-eyed pedestrians
stranded on its surface.

My heart is the cat that entertains a caress
until startled by its own pulse
into biting the hand and bolting
under the bed.

My heart is an empty notebook,
naked of ink, flipping closed
against the poet's ravishing gaze.

Four Theories About My Ovaries

I. Deaf

Dear ovaries, can you hear me? For weeks
my pituitary has been screaming hormone
louder and louder, and still you don't
respond. I imagine you
twiddling your proverbial thumbs
as you wait patiently for instructions that never
seem to come. You're just starting to wonder
if you should look for other work.

II. Temperamental

I should have known that they would be
fussy artists like myself. In adolescence,
they were daring, releasing one egg after another
to an admiring reproductive system.
But as they've aged, the self-doubt,
the perfectionism have set in.
They are embarrassed by their haphazard
early work. Anxious that the eggs
they make will be ridiculous, they lie still
praying for precise inspiration to create
the perfect ovum.

III. Retired

Susanna, lookit—we're pooped. We've been doing
this gig since you were, what, fourteen? Every
month: *pop* *pop*! We're over it! We consider
our fortune made, like young tech entrepreneurs.
From now on, you'll find us kicked back on the banks
of Fallopia, sipping luteinizing cocktails, rubbing balm
into our achy follicles.

IV.

My ovaries are not craftsmen, not businessmen
or drones. They are not even poets.
But don't call them *failure* or *vestige*.
Call them monks, eating from begging bowls
of artificial estrogen. Call them a pair of Pisces,
afloat in my abdomen, forever dreaming.

Medusa

There are conflicting stories of her origin.
She was born a scaly, serpent-headed monster,
or she started as a lovely maid.
She was virtuous or vain,
raped or wanton with the god Poseidon.

We know for sure that Athena took her severed head,
her frozen cry of fury and still-writhing snakes,
and mounted it on her shield to augment her own divine power,
a flat-handed thump to her war chest.

I look at the forked tongues of my hair's split ends,
the dull smudge of mascara below my eyes
and speckle of toothpaste on my shirt.
What a weakling I am, never daring to be truly hideous;
smiling sweetly and dangling silver from my ears
lest I should turn a man to stone.

Hangover

"Seriously, I'm over" says the Irishman. Your purse is on the couch, missing sock another matter. You are not familiar with his phrase, give a prickly: *what?* His bedroom refrigerator hums, and what's it doing there anyway? Chilled limbs of foolish girls like you? Rubs his eyes, tugs up the sheet, "seriously am over," a brogue like tangled ivy. The fridge more likely beer and mustard. You slip your naked foot inside your boot, are not familiar with this phrase. "I have no idea what you're saying" and leave, no numbers or promises exchanged.

Of course, he's "seriously hungover," you silly, sensitive girl, and you are too, so no blame for being touchy. Find a coffee shop on your way to the bus. Chamomile tea, an egg sandwich, the smile of the girl at the counter all soothe you, bruised adventurer. Your smile spreads slowly like the light that warms the morning air.

Astrology I

If he had understood the word *Virgo*, he may not have misapprehended me from the start. But astrology confirmed what I'd suspected all along: that he was too wild, while I have myself on this short leash that only lets me a little way into the future; that we were "star-crossed" which makes me think "cross-eyed," gazes falling only on our own short-lived desires.

Old ladies wear scarves on their heads to indicate that they are old ladies. I wear glasses so you'll know exactly what kind of girl I am, and yet…with all these planets whizzing around, all these constellations lost in the light of the obvious sun, who can say just what I really am? Who knows what sort of language you speak, sitting with your laptop at the kitchen table, your blue reflection gazing back from the window glass as the moon rises silently beyond the frame?

be bunny he burly

Be bunny, he burly—a bear.
Taken to arms, what's love got to do?
Treads its own tale; he is buff
and we bluster.

Don't hoppit too close, Miss Twitch.
Be soft in your warren; warrant
your nuzzling muzzle.

Be bunny. He burly. Big noises
put grizzly on edge.
Hide quiet in hedgerow
like good bunnies do.

Crochet him a note,
reject his blanket chest and then
unravel—little loops pull loose, release—
see bear's unwary hands bend books,
more nervous than a worried rabbit's foot.

See each meeting become thicket,
tongues thicken, ground tricky
with trip wires, snares...

Fuck that. Buck bunny silence,
be brave. Bear bends books,
bunny shreds them.
Be gleeful,
be weasel,
he air.

Apology

You've got that stab-eyed sweetness, apologizing
for some tiny thing. I know what it's like to see black birds
between us and to want to turn them into smoke.

We'll both be lonely this snowstorm—you with the sad
Vaudeville of your roommates; me with an empty house
and an internet I.V.

It's better this way, because: look at me—
I'm writing again! And you—you've got your feelers
feeling in a new direction.

You didn't need to apologize—I wasn't angry;
I was only teasing you for being a tree
with so many daring branches
and so many stubborn roots.

Astrology II

Your tongue falls still, moon in Cancer butting up hard against
Mercury in your third house. Rain coming down beyond my drink
and our births as caught in the cross-hairs of the stars. This quincunx
explains why I confuse fear with prescience, but not the red velvet
couches in this bar, our first tryst.

My mother is appalled, an appalling way to explain you. But Neptune
colliding with Leo in your fourth house perfectly describes a man
who will ply me with pomegranate cocktails. Who will jump out of
bed to make breakfast wearing only one blue sock.

You said "horseshit" but then you had to ask. It's true: moon in Pisces
so I'm vast like the ocean but slippery like fishes. The rain drenches
but it doesn't stick.

Wash my mouth with astrophysics. I'm tired and I can't afford
another drink. Mercury's coming back around, and your silence is just
the space between Venus and the sun.

on disgruntle to westminster

Damned organic urban development, bad as Boston. Only to Trafalgar and I'm missing the guard, they've started. On disgruntle to Westminster—fly, my buttress! To be on the walk when the clock strikes—only One, alas. He says Big Bell shakes him like a quake but I'm stuck unmoved, moated—nasty traffic circle, distract me to the impossible square. I believe in tele-transportation, disavow "subways." I believe in flying monks above their municipal placards all unawares, and that our magnets flip, flip—repel, attract, dispel, enact. We fit the Brits, our signage over-polite, verbose, invisibly indignant.

Whose disgruntle is this? Perhaps of the chicken whose breast was breaded into my bad lunch. Or belongs to the fear of heights striking me between the paws of a bronze lion, or oceans sore of those driven across them—back and froth, or rather, sea foam, disappointed mermaids.

Light in the grated cloister is still glad and crenellations chiseled in rose and unicorn. Magpies I know their names, Gargle and Wordless. Chiaroscuro clouds gearing for Friday's storm (when cloister will turn verb, discomfort. Rain and an £8 admission, or else I'd church it. Solitude the third in our triangle.)

But let's stick to Wednesday when sun cut the slatey sky. A hawk-holding pigeon-stomper back at Trafalgar. Fountain spray ridiculing the surface of my spectacles but not without, first, drawing a weak rainbow against the light; drawing a subtle sigh.

for reptilian or nutcrack

Forever at 5:30 AM will the house-munchers arrive.
Morse code, small rain, small fires they speak
from the walls.

The mouse king sleeps, bides time.
At night when I'm shrunk he wraps his pointed fingers
around my arm, breathes yellow past terrible incisors,
air of cheese and rancid meat hot against my cheek.

Arrives my dull hero, the nut-chomping soldier,
and cuts a red swath through matted fur.
The king's whiskers graze my forehead
as he turns, flees, thrashing a wrathful tale.
Nutcrack clacks his jaw.

Daytime, the king's minions fit through impossible dime-holes.
He teaches them snap trap and glue pool.
They fetch his oats and fat scraps,
leaving evidence to taunt us.

At night his wet nose to my ear, I loathe him,
but Nutcrack, my savior, is no better,
insists on visiting rich friends,
their international treasures,
their saccharin décor.

Oh for an impregnable fortress.

Oh for a snake with a bulge in its middle.

Hither

"Come on in here with me," *he crooned.* "I've got a sizzling stovetop and a kitchen clapper"

Me: I do not know what you said.

He puckers up. He whistled. "Don't be so obtuse, my aubergine, with your Dutch bottom, your plum-dunn sheath."

Me: Am I to be your vegetable?
"Don't go all nightshade, love." *He winks. He batted.* "Come toasty now. I got a whoooole jar o' marmalade."

Me *(staying planted in the other room):* . . .

He come-hithered. He finger curls. "I'm in here, baby, with this rigid fridge, a warm agar bath. It staggers the imagination. I'll be down on hands and knees! I'll clap the kitchen just for you!"

Me: Your doorway smells of vinegar and you look like uncooked meat. Clap that kitchen all you want—I won't applause. I'm no house-mouse, no flour, nor courgette. I'll cook my own jams down to savor sweet. I exit. Bon appetite.

Moving In

I'm moving to a new apartment
with my boyfriend. It's time
to pack everything. Books and books and books
in mid-sized boxes. Notebooks from graduate school
that I hope to read again, sometime,
to refresh my professional prowess.
Framed posters and pictures
(Maybe I'll get real art some day).

I pack new clothes and clothes with holes.
I pack earrings I bought in high school and earrings
he gave me last year. I pack toothpaste.
I pack pens and umbrellas and water bottles.
I pack unopened packs of chewing gum,
and every single mug.

I pack my boyfriend. I wrap him in bubble wrap
and roll him in blankets and load him onto the truck,
nestled between the sofa and the mattress where he'll be safe.

At the new place, I bring up the furniture first,
set it up nicely. I set the boxes in neat stacks.
At last, I unwrap him and sit him gently on the couch
and hand him a cup of tea.

I tell him "This is where we live now! What do you think?"
"Not bad," he says, with a cautious smile. Then,
smile broadening, "Not bad at all!"

I hand him his favorite book, which I packed at the top
of the nearest box: *A People's History of the United States*.
I ask him to read aloud to me as I rest my head
against his shoulder, stocking feet tucked beneath me.
This is home.

My Husband

is the square root of my in-laws.
He does not recognize that he
is them, distilled.

His mother he derides as
Social Justice the Hedgehog,
yet he himself subsists on little
but cage-free mangoes
and fair-trade moon pies;
moons over Ralph Nader;
provokes our conservative neighbors
with tirades about the plight
of the greater sage-grouse
then curls into a woeful
prickled ball when the neighbors
tirade back.

His father he has dubbed
Raptor, the Tutelary Pigeon.
"Sit Raptor, sit!" he'll whisper
from the side of his mouth
as his plump, beaky dad
falls asleep standing up
at his nightly watch for wolves,
burglars, goblins, peeping toms

and Mongol hoards.

Yet my husband himself
often sleepwalks to the
bedroom window and braces
the frame with his broad arms,
daring the night: *just try—*
just try to frighten my wife
with your pitchy unknown.
You'll never get past me.

Dream Life

We were in Argentina
   (but it was my parents' dining room)
and they had a cat
   (but it was a wild fox)
and you were you
   (but you were also my high school nemesis)
and we were eating lobster
   (but it was a pile of sticks)
and I was wearing a cable-knit sweater
   (but somehow my boobs were exposed)
and I'd forgotten my lines
   (but the play was only a joke)
and my knees didn't work
   (but we all moved by somersaults)
and my phone wouldn't work
   (but it kept making that noise)
and my eyes were stuck shut
   (it was time to wake up)
and I was lying in bed
   (I was lying in bed)
and my eyes came open
and you were snoring softly beside me
and yet I had left you behind, all the way back
in Argentina.

Love

When Giles insisted he was pregnant,
and the moon grew frothy with our love,
the Truth was like a squish-squash of sea foam,
so pretty, and unfixed.

The bumble bees kept coming to our garden.
I used to prefer them, and now
I *am* one, slurping at boundless sweetness
and building up a pair of gold-grained pantaloons.

Giles joshes that I am a harem girl,
but I remind him that pollen is the palanquin
of the *male* gamete. I'm more sultan
than slave girl, as he should well know,
full as he is with child; our little bumble-bun
in the oven, seed of the apple of my eye.

Quake

Prologue

Some days I eschew the subway which might
cave in and kill us in an earthquake,
and stay, instead, in buildings
which might fall in and kill us
in an earthquake.

I have a friend who'd like to die by earthquake
or ninjas, but I
find terror distasteful.

Wind gusting around the corners makes a ruckus,
shakes the house like a little quake.
I'm safe in this Now, plaster intact, dishes quiet in their cabinets.
Today there's just wind, and walls will protect me from that monster
that's got all the trash cans moaning on their backs,
forgetting themselves.

     *   *   *

Words of the Day

parse

The innocent ground, in miles-wide chunks, rubs
against itself, not knowing it has the power to shake a building
into its component parts and make them deadly:
cornice, soffit, pane,
brick and brick, and cladding stone,
rebar protruding like ruptured bone.

Modifier presses and shifts against noun
and the sentence settles into place with a quake.

jeremiad

O woe is me the quake will come and kill us all and I shall die
single, and unpublished, or not die
but lose my writing arm and live to see my friends perish
or publish and I'll be stricken with either grief
or envy.

supine

In the grass at Yerba Buena park,
the sky so blue—my slice of open air, my eavesdrop screen—
"He gets this look on his face like he wants to do me harm;
like he's about to hurt me and enjoy it and I find it

incredibly hot."
The well of sky holds tower tops at a distance;
they can't hurt you here.

befitting
What is a good way for a poet to die?
A man on the hiking trail reveals
that Frank O'Hara perished after being struck by a beach buggy.
"Plunging off this precipice," says the hiker,
indicating the drop to our right,
"that would be a better death for a poet."

fractious
A fault line just itching for a fight.

raffish
The dishes are quiet in their cabinets, but perhaps
the ground is not as innocent as it appears, a wolf
in turf's clothing, a vulgar rake. Stays quiet 'til we think
he's drunk himself dead, then suddenly arrives at the party,
turns the music way up, breaks bottles, gropes girls,
and everyone howls in outrage, yet can't help
but to love him. To lay down with him, the Ground,
in the very end. He looks at me like he wants

to do me harm.

brackish

The seismologists have yet to discover this truth:
Our hearts throb, endeavor to break free of our bodies
and love every last member of the human race.
But our hearts dare not leave us for fear of killing our bodies
and so they endeavor as well to check their own violent escape.
And this tension, between the riot and the stillness,
is transmitted as vibration through our bodies
to the ground which amplifies it, shimmies and buckles
and shakes loose our tears which become oceans,
which are pushed ashore in tsunami by the writhing earth,
and thus will humanity drown itself through the suppression
of its own self-love.

limpid

San Francisco's Marina district is built on landfill which drifts
into the aquatic park and muddies the bay.
This may or may not be a complete fabrication,
a lie. Like the clear pools that are your eyes; in truth,
I can't even tell you their color. And in my dreams
they are windows that open
not onto the soul, but onto opaque
curtains, always drawn.

specious
Falling boulders. My friends agree—
that's the way to go.

cogitate
Oh death, where is thy sting?
Over there, over there, like flies;
in headlines and the pit of my stomach.
It's far too much for the page.
Let me speak of deaths that *could* be
rather than of deaths that *are*.
The best I can do is to live in my moment
which is forever grasping at the future.
In these troubled times, what are our responsibilities as writers?
My neighbor's dog takes a moment from her frolic
to push her hard round head into my palm. Her vocation
is to tear across the lawn, and be loved.

stasis
The city will fall down. I stretch my hands out, willing it to stay up.
Stay, I tell it. *Stay!*

terror
There are those who want to hurt us
(*whom do they love?*)
An old friend intends to leave New York, fearing terrorists
and I intend to leave San Francisco, fearing earthquakes.
Maybe we'll meet somewhere in the heartland,
see if we can find its namesake:
tough red muscle, elusive organ.

We *intend* to leave but find ourselves still
at America's extremities; her hands. Paused
with pen above paper waiting for a jolt
to action.

appellation
I dreamt I was unsaying my name (*"subanna…bubaha…"*)
until it was nearly divorced from me
and I was in danger of losing myself.

trepidation
Well, that one goes without saying:
My trembling fear:
of walking into a room and finding the wrong person there;
of waking in a room that has crumbled and dissipated;
of working in a room until the pages are all [empty].

methodical

Today I put papers in neat piles.
All my Virgo grasp and file cannot forestall—

taciturn

Sometimes I manage to hold my tongue,
do not Cassandra death and disaster.
Sometimes we maintain radio silence
until the static prickles our skin
and our limbs fall dead asleep,
that they may wake refreshed.

somnolence

My co-spooner wakes with a grunt, aborted snore
that is the means to its own end, and tightens
his tender grip around me;
then drifts back to sleep and his arms
go loose again and again he snorts softly awake…
So that I am drifting too, in the waves of his embrace;
No great romance, but a kind of grace.

profligate

The dissolute plaster falling in chunks,
dishes toppling to the ground.

profligate
Is this town more reckless and sinful,
anticipating its imminent destruction?

profligate
Remember that time when I jumped
to the conclusion that my friend was dying?
I was living with my knees slightly bent,
ready for tragedy from any direction.

resolute
All this wind can't shake loose the green kick-ball
stuck for months in the branches of my neighbor's tree.

oblation
The graceful sweep of the hand with which the office girl
catches the slender cord and pulls the little earphone from her ear
to hear us.

The full moon painting its long white reflection
on the ocean, past the runway of streetlights.

The quaint covered reservoir, seismically reinforced.
The seagulls above it, rising on their thin, flat arms.

Ode

for Brendan

You are so even-tempered, as if
healthful minerals ran in your tributaries
or you could meander through
the narrow straits of the harbor
to get to the chamber orchestra.

You read about history because you
appreciate it. As if it weren't enough
that you sing in churches
and dance like a housecat, you
have to think I am a great woman!

and I stride distractedly by on my
convoluted mission, determined like a flock of geese.
Thinking you a simple landmark. Acting
awfully selfish. But you are wide-eyed
again, shouting cheerful hellos at your little nephew.

I must remember: a steady, handsome tenor
is full of comfort. Be always easy,
full of Chapsticks and ice cream and loose change. Oh
ride your bike in green sunshine, be joyful!
and wear my affection, because it suits you.

—

About the Poet

Susanna Kittredge's poems have appeared in publications such as *Barrow Street, 14 Hills, The Columbia Review,* and *Salamander* as well as the anthologies *Bay Poetics* (Faux Press, 2006) and *Shadowed: Unheard Voices* (The Press at California State University, Fresno 2014). She holds an MFA in Creative Writing from San Francisco State University. She currently lives in the Boston area and is an active member of The Jamaica Pond Poets workshop group and the Brighton Word Factory, a bi-weekly open writing group. By day she teaches academic skills to eighth graders.

Made in the USA
Coppell, TX
24 January 2020